The True Vine Reflection Journal 1

Apart from Him, We Can Do Nothing

Evangelist Danena L. Williams

Cadmus Publishing
www.cadmuspublishing.com

Copyright © Danena L. Williams

Published by Cadmus Publishing
www.cadmuspublishing.com
Port Angeles, WA

ISBN: 978-1-63751-239-5
Library of Congress Control Number: 2022917486

All rights reserved. Copyright under Berne Copyright Convention, Universal Copyright Convention, and Pan-American Copyright Convention. No part of this book may be reproduced, stored in a retrieval system, or transmitted in any form, or by any means, electronic, mechanical, photocopying, recording or otherwise, without prior permission of the author.

Unless otherwise noted, Scripture quotations are taken from the New American Standard Bible (NASB) Copyright 1960, 1962, 1963, 1968, 1971, 1972, 1973, 1975, 1977, 1995 by the Lockman Foundation. Used by permission.
Other Scripture quotations are from the following sources: Holy Bible, New International Version (NIV) Copyright 1973, 1978, 1984 by International Bible Society. Used by permission of Zondervan. All rights reserved. Common English Bible (CEB) Copyright 2011. Used by permission. All right reserved. Holman Christian Standard Bible (HCSB) Copyright 1999, 2000, 2002, 2003, 2009 by Holman Bible Publishers. Used by permission. New Living Translation (NLT) Copyright 1996, 2004, 2015 by Tyndale House Publishers, Inc. Carol Stream, Illinois 60188. All rights reserved. English Standard Version (ESV) Copyright 2001 by Crossway, a publishing ministry of Good News Publishers. Used by permission. All rights reserved. New King James Version (NKJV) Copyright 1979, 1980, 1982 by Thomas Nelson, Inc. Used by permission. All rights reserved.

Don't Let Go

When the world is cold and harsh,
the pressures of life grip you by the throat.

When depression no longer subsides,
sadness and fear hoist you up,
while anxieties arise.

When your emotions are roaring and raging,
the mind suffers in a state of delirium.

When shadows of your storms encase you,
allowing tears to suffocate you,
misery becomes your crypt.

When you can't hold on any longer,
your spirit is broken and tired.

When you're lost and seeking relief,
dig deep and hold on to your belief.

Don't let go... just hold on to God!

Co-Written By: Danena Williams and Desiree Carter

THE TRUE VINE - REFLECTION JOURNAL 1

Day 1

Stay Connected and Bear Fruit

Scripture Reading
John 15:1-7

Reflection
    Take the time to examine your life today. Are you connected to the vine? Are you bearing fruit?

THE TRUE VINE - REFLECTION JOURNAL 1

Day 2

Heavenly Bread

Scripture Reading
Matthew 6:11 and Exodus 16:4 and Philippians 4:19

Reflection
God's supply of blessings is unlimited. All you have to do is ask. What do you need to ask Jesus for today?

THE TRUE VINE - REFLECTION JOURNAL 1

Day 3

Thirst No More

Scripture Reading
John 4:3-14; 7:38

Reflection
Will you continue to drink from the well or will you accept Christ's offer of "living water" today and never thirst again?

THE TRUE VINE - REFLECTION JOURNAL 1

Day 4

Letters To God

Scripture Reading
Psalm 23

Reflection
Write your own prayer to God. Tell Him what's on your heart.

THE TRUE VINE - REFLECTION JOURNAL 1

Day 5

His Creation / His Glory

Scripture Reading
John 1:1-3 and Genesis 1

Reflection
On your next outing, stop for a moment, and take a look around you. Do you see God's glory?

THE TRUE VINE - REFLECTION JOURNAL 1

Day 6

Fruits Of The Spirit - Love

Scripture Reading
Galatians 5:22-23 and 1 Corinthians 13:4-8

Reflection
If you ever find yourself needing a refresher course on love, the Bible has hundreds of lessons and references about this fruit of the spirit. Pray and ask God to fill you with His perfect love so that you may share it with the world.

THE TRUE VINE - REFLECTION JOURNAL 1

Day 7

Tested but not Broken

Scripture Reading
Job 1-2

Reflection
How has God allowed you to be tested? How was God protecting you through your test?

THE TRUE VINE - REFLECTION JOURNAL 1

Day 8

12 Ordinary Men - Matthew

Scripture Reading
Mark 2:17 and Matthew 9:9-13; 10:1-4

Reflection
The disciples are prime examples of how God can and will work through any person who is willing to do the work of God. Are you a willing vessel? If so, how have you allowed God to use you? If not, will you choose today to allow God to work through you?

THE TRUE VINE - REFLECTION JOURNAL 1

Day 9

Declare and Decree - You Are A Child of God

Scripture Reading
John 14:1-4 and Romans 8:37-39

Reflection
Write your own declaration, and speak it over your life.

THE TRUE VINE - REFLECTION JOURNAL 1

Day 10

Never Alone

Scripture Reading
Joshua 1: 1-8 and John 14:16-17

Reflection
Embark on a new journey, take that 90 day challenge, ask for a promotion, do the things you've always wanted to do knowing that you are destined for success. Create a plan of action and get started today.

THE TRUE VINE - REFLECTION JOURNAL 1

DANENA L. WILLIAMS

THE TRUE VINE - REFLECTION JOURNAL 1

Day 11

On Good Ground

Scripture Reading
Mark 4:1-20

Reflection
When we receive the Word of God, we must plant it deep within our hearts, meditate on it day and night, and allow it to manifest in our actions, speech, and daily lives. Do you see manifestation of God's word in your life? If not, consider what kind of ground your seeds are falling on.

THE TRUE VINE - REFLECTION JOURNAL 1

Day 12

Letters To God

Scripture Reading
John 15:12-14 and Isaiah 12:2

Reflection
Write your own prayer to God. Tell Him what's on your heart.

THE TRUE VINE - REFLECTION JOURNAL 1

Day 13

The Power of Testimony

Scripture Reading
Revelation 12:11 and Acts 22, 26

Reflection
There's no time like the present, start writing down your story today, and start actively looking for opportunities to share your testimony.

THE TRUE VINE - REFLECTION JOURNAL 1

Day 14

Fruits Of The Spirit - Joy

Scripture Reading
Galatians 5:22-23 and Proverbs 17:22 and John 16:24

Reflection
Remember that the joy of the Lord is yours. It dwells inside you. Therefore, rejoice in all things big and small. Can you think of a time when you experienced the joy of the Lord?

THE TRUE VINE - REFLECTION JOURNAL 1

Day 15

Taming The Littlest Member

Scripture Reading
James 3:2-12 and Proverbs 18:21 and Matthew 12:37

Reflection
Do a moral inventory, confess your sins to God, and give Him control. He will transform your heart, and your speech will reflect that transformation. Will you decide today to tame your littlest member?

THE TRUE VINE - REFLECTION JOURNAL 1

Day 16

Step out on Faith

Scripture Reading
Matthew 14:22-33

Reflection
What storms in your life have caused you to take your eyes off Jesus? In the future, how do you plan to step out on Faith?

THE TRUE VINE - REFLECTION JOURNAL 1

Day 17

12 Ordinary Men - Simon Peter and Andrew

Scripture Reading
Mark 2:17 and Matthew 10:1-4 and John 1:35-42

Reflection

    The disciples are prime examples of how God can and will work through any person who is willing to do the work of God. Are you a willing vessel? If so, how have you allowed God to use you? If not, will you choose today to allow God to work through you?

THE TRUE VINE - REFLECTION JOURNAL 1

Day 18

Authentic Love

Scripture Reading
1 Corinthians 13:4-8 and Songs of Songs 1-8

Reflection
Solomon's song teaches us what real love is and where it originates. Take some time to consider this teaching. Has this song changed your perspective of love? If so, how?

THE TRUE VINE - REFLECTION JOURNAL 1

Day 19

Serenity Prayer

Scripture Reading
Matthew 6:10 and Philippians 4:11-13

Reflection
Write your own prayer to God. Tell Him what's on your heart.

THE TRUE VINE - REFLECTION JOURNAL 1

Day 20

Humble in Spirit

Scripture Reading
Luke 1:26-38

Reflection
Are you willing to serve God in the face of adversity?

THE TRUE VINE - REFLECTION JOURNAL 1

DANENA L. WILLIAMS

THE TRUE VINE - REFLECTION JOURNAL 1

Day 21

Once Lost but Now Found

Scripture Reading
Luke 15:11-32

Reflection
Will you repent of your sins today and accept your Father's forgiveness, love, grace, and mercy?

THE TRUE VINE - REFLECTION JOURNAL 1

Day 22

One Of A Kind

Scripture Reading
John 1:14 and Hebrews 11:17 and Psalms 139:13-14

Reflection
God created you, uniquely you, and you are precious to Him. So, embrace who you are, and be unapologetically you. List some of the characteristics that make you, You!

THE TRUE VINE - REFLECTION JOURNAL 1

Day 23

Declare and Decree - You Are An Overcomer

Scripture Reading
John 16:33

Reflection
Write your own declaration, and speak it over your life.

THE TRUE VINE - REFLECTION JOURNAL 1

Day 24

Deny Your Flesh

Scripture Reading
1 Peter 2:11 and Romans 8:5-9

Reflection
Can you think of a situation when consulting with your spirit would have kept you out of trouble? Journal about what happened and what you could have done differently.

THE TRUE VINE - REFLECTION JOURNAL 1

Day 25

Fruits Of The Spirit - Peace

Scripture Reading
Galatians 5:22-33 and Philippians 4:7

Reflection
When your life seems to be in disarray, retreat to the peaceful bosom of the Lord. Find solace in God's presence. Journal and describe what this sense of peace feels like to you.

THE TRUE VINE - REFLECTION JOURNAL 1

Day 26

Plans of Prosperity

Scripture Reading
Jeremiah 29: 4-7, 10-14

Reflection
Can you turn control over to God and let Him implement His plan for your life?

THE TRUE VINE - REFLECTION JOURNAL 1

Day 27

Letters To God

Scripture Reading
Genesis 1:26-27

Reflection
Write your own prayer to God. Tell Him what's on your heart.

THE TRUE VINE - REFLECTION JOURNAL 1

Day 28

Using Your Gift

Scripture Reading
Romans 12:6-8 and 1 Corinthians 12:4-11

Reflection
Do a self evaluation of your spiritual strengths. Ask the Holy Spirit to reveal your gifts to you. Begin to study and learn about your gift or gifts. Journal about each step of this process.

THE TRUE VINE - REFLECTION JOURNAL 1

Day 29

12 Ordinary Men - Judas

Scripture Reading
Mark 2:17 and Matthew 10:1-4 and John 6:70-71

Reflection
The disciples are prime examples of how God can and will work through any person who is willing to do the work of God. Are you a willing vessel? If so, how have you allowed God to use you? If not, will you choose today to allow God to work through you?

THE TRUE VINE - REFLECTION JOURNAL 1

Day 30

The Fiery Furnace

Scripture Reading
Daniel 3

Reflection
What furnace are you facing currently? Do you believe that God will allow you to come out on the other side without a singe?

THE TRUE VINE - REFLECTION JOURNAL 1

DANENA L. WILLIAMS

THE TRUE VINE - REFLECTION JOURNAL 1

Jesus Got Jokes

There was a preacher who fell into the ocean and couldn't swim. When a boat came by, the captain yelled, "Hey! Do you need help?". The preacher calmly replied, "No, God will save me." A little while later, another boat came by and a fisherman yelled, "Sir, Do you need help?". Again the preacher calmly said, " No, God will save me." Eventually, the preacher drowned and went to heaven. When he got there the preacher asked God, "Why didn't you save me?". God replied, "Well, I sent you two boats".

Jesus Got Jokes

#1 Q: Who was the greatest financier in the Bible?

A: Noah. He was floating his stock while everyone else was in liquidation.

#2 If you look up the word "rib" in the dictionary, It says "To vex, irritate, or annoy." If you look up the word "rib" in the Bible, It says "Woman". Coincidence?

#3 Q: What did Jonah's family say when he told them about the predicament he got himself into?

A: "Hmm, sounds fishy!"

#4 Q: What kind of car would Jesus drive?

A: A Christler.

Day 31

Declare and Decree - You Are Blessed

Scripture Reading
Psalm 1:1, 32:1-2

Reflection
Write your own declaration, and speak it over your life.

THE TRUE VINE - REFLECTION JOURNAL 1

Day 32

Joy

Scripture Reading
Romans 15:13 and Psalm 30:5

Reflection
Do you want to experience true everlasting joy; the kind that Paul spoke of in Corinthians? Will you allow God to be your source?

THE TRUE VINE - REFLECTION JOURNAL 1

Day 33

Fruits Of The Spirit - Longsuffering/Patience

Scripture Reading
Galatians 5:22-23 and Psalm 40:1 and James 5:7-8

Reflection
If you find yourself in a situation that is testing your patience, remind yourself of all the times God was patient with you. Then, do what God would... exhibit patient endurance.

THE TRUE VINE - REFLECTION JOURNAL 1

Day 34

IN NEED OF A SPIRITUAL REFILL

Scripture Reading
Acts 3:19 and Isaiah 40:31

Reflection
Journal about a time when you were spiritually drained. Then, spend some time in the presence of God. Allow Him to refill and renew your spirit.

THE TRUE VINE - REFLECTION JOURNAL 1

Day 35

Letters To God

Scripture Reading
Romans 15:13

Reflection
Write your own prayer to God. Tell Him what's on your heart.

THE TRUE VINE - REFLECTION JOURNAL 1

DANENA L. WILLIAMS

DAY 36

FOR YOUR GOOD

Scripture Reading
Romans 8:28-31

Reflection
Can you think of a time when a situation was supposed to be a negative for you, but some how ended up being a positive? Could you tell that God had stepped in and turned things around? If so, how?

THE TRUE VINE - REFLECTION JOURNAL 1

Day 37

12 Ordinary Men - James and John

Scripture Reading
Mark 2:17 and Matthew 4:21-22; 10:1-4

Reflection
The disciples are prime examples of how God can and will work through any person who is willing to do the work of God. Are you a willing vessel? If so, how have you allowed God to use you? If not, will you choose today to allow God to work through you?

THE TRUE VINE - REFLECTION JOURNAL 1

Day 38

Reap What You Sow

Scripture Reading
Galatians 6:6-10 and 2 Corinthians 9:6 and Job 4:8

Reflection
What has your harvest looked like lately? Are you sowing positivity or negativity, good or evil, truth or lies, success or failure?

THE TRUE VINE - REFLECTION JOURNAL 1

Day 39

Declare and Decree - You are Patient

Scripture Reading
Hebrews 10:35-36

Reflection
Write your own declaration, and speak it over your life.

THE TRUE VINE - REFLECTION JOURNAL 1

Day 40

Answer Jesus' Call

Scripture Reading
1 Corinthians 7:24 and Matthew 20:28; 26:39

Reflection
You must serve God faithfully no matter the circumstances. Even Jesus was required to stay in his current situation, despite His discomfort, in order to serve the purpose God had sent Him for. Are you willing to make the best of your situation and circumstances in order to serve the purpose God has called you for?

THE TRUE VINE - REFLECTION JOURNAL 1

THE TRUE VINE - REFLECTION JOURNAL 1

Day 41

Martha and Mary

Scripture Reading
Luke 10:38-42 and Deuteronomy 8:3

Reflection
We must take special time out of our day to allow the Holy Spirit to minister to us. Will you commit today to spending more time in the presence of God?

THE TRUE VINE - REFLECTION JOURNAL 1

Day 42

Hannah's Prayer of Praise

Scripture Reading
1 Samuel 2:1-10 and Psalm 62:11

Reflection
Write your own prayer to God. Tell Him what's on your heart.

THE TRUE VINE - REFLECTION JOURNAL 1

Day 43

Bless This Land

Scripture Reading
Jeremiah 29:4-7 and Isaiah 32:15-18

Reflection

Scripture tells us that God's spirit can transform the wilderness into a peaceful, fertile dwelling place. So imagine what He can do for your city, town, etc... Will you commit today to pray for the land that you inhabit? What changes would you like to see? After you pray, create a plan of action and start bringing about change.

THE TRUE VINE - REFLECTION JOURNAL 1

Day 44

The Good Samaritan

Scripture Reading
Luke 6:27-31; 10:30-37

Reflection
Are you willing to take a lesson from the good Samaritan? Will you allow yourself to have concern for others that knows no bounds?

THE TRUE VINE - REFLECTION JOURNAL 1

Day 45

Fruits Of The Spirit - Kindness

Scripture Reading
Galatians 5:22-23 and Ephesians 4:31-32 and Lamentations 3:22

Reflection
Everyone is created in Gods image and deserves to be treated with compassion, tenderness, grace, love, and mercy. So, as you go about your daily activities, treat everyone you encounter as Jesus would. Then, journal about your experiences.

THE TRUE VINE - REFLECTION JOURNAL 1

Day 46

Temptation

Scripture Reading
Matthew 4:1-11; 6:18

Reflection
We must resist the devil and his wicked temptations. We must be spiritually prepared at all times. How do you feel you could better prepare yourself for the attacks of the enemy?

THE TRUE VINE - REFLECTION JOURNAL 1

DAY 47

12 ORDINARY MEN - THOMAS

Scripture Reading
Mark 2:17 and Matthew 10:1-4 and John 20:19-29

Reflection
The disciples are prime examples of how God can and will work through any person who is willing to do the work of God. Are you a willing vessel? If so, how have you allowed God to use you? If not, will you choose today to allow God to work through you?

THE TRUE VINE - REFLECTION JOURNAL 1

Day 48

Accomplished

Scripture Reading
1 Kings 1:28-37; 3:3-13 and 2 Samuel 11-12

Reflection
Just as He did for Solomon, God will give you the wisdom and knowledge that you need to accomplish great things. What do you want to accomplish? Ask God today for the knowledge and wisdom needed to fulfill your dreams.

THE TRUE VINE - REFLECTION JOURNAL 1

Day 49

Letters to God

Scripture Reading
Matthew 6:25-26, 32-33

Reflection
Write your own prayer to God. Tell Him what's on your heart.

THE TRUE VINE - REFLECTION JOURNAL 1

Day 50

Casting Stone

Scripture Reading
John 8:1-11

Reflection
Can you think of a time when the angry mob was pointing the finger at you? or maybe a time when you were leading an angry mob against someone else? How has your perspective of things changed today?

THE TRUE VINE - REFLECTION JOURNAL 1

Day 51

Give

Scripture Reading
2 Corinthians 7-11

Reflection
We must train our spiritual eye to see what a person needs, and then provide for them according to our Father's riches and glory. Pray for God to bless you in abundance so that you can care for His children in need. For this is pleasing to God.

THE TRUE VINE - REFLECTION JOURNAL 1

Day 52

Fruits Of The Spirit - Goodness

Scripture Reading
Galatians 5:22-23 and Psalm 23:6

Reflection
As we go through life, we must be self aware and conscious of the image we project. Strive to have praise worthy characteristics and exhibit moral excellence at all times. Journal about your characteristics and whether or not they're praise worthy.

THE TRUE VINE - REFLECTION JOURNAL 1

Day 53

Just Say No

Scripture Reading
Jeremiah 17:14 and Psalm 6:2-4, 8-9

Reflection
Make a conscious decision today to turn your addiction over to Christ. Will you believe Him for your healing?

THE TRUE VINE - REFLECTION JOURNAL 1

Day 54

Declare and Decree - You Are Favored

Scripture Reading
Psalm 8:35; 5:12; 37:4; 106:4

Reflection
Write your own declaration, and speak it over your life.

THE TRUE VINE - REFLECTION JOURNAL 1

Day 55

Growth

Scripture Reading
Luke 2:52 and James 1:5 and Proverbs 1:2-5

Reflection
In what areas of your life do you need to acquire more knowledge? What would you like to study or learn in the future? Ask God to start increasing your knowledge today.

THE TRUE VINE - REFLECTION JOURNAL 1

Day 56

12 Ordinary Men - Judas the son of James

Scripture Reading
Mark 2:17 and Matthew 10:1-4 and John 14:22

Reflection

The disciples are prime examples of how God can and will work through any person who is willing to do the work of God. Are you a willing vessel? If so, how have you allowed God to use you? If not, will you choose today to allow God to work through you?

THE TRUE VINE - REFLECTION JOURNAL 1

Day 57

Shine

Scripture Reading
Matthew 5:16 and Romans 12:9-21

Reflection
Take some time to consider your daily actions. Are you following Paul's instructions? Do you behave like a Christian?

THE TRUE VINE - REFLECTION JOURNAL 1

Day 58

Letters To God

Scripture Reading
2 Corinthians 5:7 and Psalm 25:4-5

Reflection
Write your own prayer to God. Tell Him what's on your heart.

THE TRUE VINE - REFLECTION JOURNAL 1

Day 59

Good Religious Practices

Scripture Reading
Matthew 6:1-4, 5-8, 16-18

Reflection
One would be correct to assume that the good religious practices of giving, fasting, and praying are a matter of the heart between the Christian and God. Journal your thoughts on this subject.

THE TRUE VINE - REFLECTION JOURNAL 1

Day 60

The Company You Keep

Scripture Reading
2 Corinthians 6:14 and Proverbs 13:20 and 1 Corinthians 15:33

Reflection
Take the time to do a moral inventory of the people you are yoked with. Do you entertain any bad company?

THE TRUE VINE - REFLECTION JOURNAL 1

DANENA L. WILLIAMS

Jesus Got Jokes

#1 Q: What did the boy say when the teacher asked him why he kept walking next to the same little girl at school?

A: "My Sunday school teacher said I'm supposed to walk by Faith!"

#2 Q: How many people can fit in one Honda?

A: Well, the Bible said that all 12 disciples were in one accord.

#3 Q: How does Moses like his coffee?

A: He-brews

#4 Q: What kind of man was Boaz before he got married?

A: Ruthless

Jesus Got Jokes

A man was talking to God:
Man: "God, how long is a million years?"
God: "To me, it's about a minute."
Man: "How much is a million dollars?"
God: "To me, it's a penny."
Man: "God, may I have a penny?"
God: "Yes, if you can wait a minute."

A scientist was talking to God:
Scientist: "We've worked out a way to make a man without you.
God: "Okay, then. Show me."
The scientist bent down and picked up a handful of dirt but God stopped him.
God: "Oh, no you don't. Create your own dirt."

Day 61

Fruits Of The Spirit - Faithfulness

Scripture Reading
Galatians 5:22-23 and Lamentations 3:23 and Psalm 36:5 and Deuteronomy 7:9

Reflection
If you are not familiar with God's promises, spend some time looking them up. The Bible is full of them. God has spoken a word to address every circumstance we may face in life. Use your journal to write down the promises that stand out to you.

THE TRUE VINE - REFLECTION JOURNAL 1

Day 62

12 Ordinary Men - Bartholomew and James

Scripture Reading
Mark 2:17 and Matthew 10:1-4 and John 1:46-49

Reflection

The disciples are prime examples of how God can and will work through any person who is willing to do the work of God. Are you a willing vessel? If so, how have you allowed God to use you? If not, will you choose today to allow God to work through you?

THE TRUE VINE - REFLECTION JOURNAL 1

Day 63

Obedience - Better Than Sacrifice

Scripture Reading
1 Kings 17:8-16

Reflection
Strive to be more like the widow. Tune your ear to hear when the Lord is summoning you, and actively respond to God's word in obedience. Journal your experiences.

THE TRUE VINE - REFLECTION JOURNAL 1

Day 64

Spiritual Purity

Scripture Reading
Matthew 5:8 and 1 Samuel 16:7

Reflection
Instead of looking in the mirror, look deep within. Soul search, and ask God to show you what you need to work on. Then strive towards being pure at heart.

THE TRUE VINE - REFLECTION JOURNAL 1

DANENA L. WILLIAMS

Day 65

Mary's Song of Praise

Scripture Reading
Luke 1:42, 46-55; 2:10-11

Reflection
Write your own prayer to God. Tell Him what's on your heart.

THE TRUE VINE - REFLECTION JOURNAL 1

Day 66

Pressed

Scripture Reading
Mark 14:38; 26:33-34 and 1 Corinthians 10:12 and Hebrews 4:15

Reflection
We have to watch and pray at all times in order to be spiritually alert because spiritual unpreparedness leads to spiritual disaster. Can you think of a time when you were spiritually unprepared to handle a situation? How would things have turned out differently if you would have been spiritually alert?

THE TRUE VINE - REFLECTION JOURNAL 1

DANENA L. WILLIAMS

Day 67

12 Ordinary Men - Simon The Zealot

Scripture Reading
Mark 2:17 and Matthew 10:1-4

Reflection
    The disciples are prime examples of how God can and will work through any person who is willing to do the work of God. Are you a willing vessel? If so, how have you allowed God to use you? If not, will you choose today to allow God to work through you?

THE TRUE VINE - REFLECTION JOURNAL 1

Day 68

Declare and Decree - You Are Victorious

Scripture Reading
Romans 8:37 and 1 Corinthians 15:57 and 1 John 5:4

Reflection
Write your own declaration, and speak it over your life.

THE TRUE VINE - REFLECTION JOURNAL 1

Day 69

Don't Blame God

Scripture Reading
Job 2:10 and Jeremiah 29:11

Reflection
How many times have you blamed God for the problems, sufferings, or obstacles you've faced in life? Journal and reflect on those occasions.

THE TRUE VINE - REFLECTION JOURNAL 1

Day 70

Don't Blame God: Reason #1

Scripture Reading
Proverbs 48:14 and Psalm 18:30

Reflection
God Uses Problems To Guide Us. Can you think of a time in your life when God changed the plan in the middle of your plans?

THE TRUE VINE - REFLECTION JOURNAL 1

THE TRUE VINE - REFLECTION JOURNAL 1

Day 71

Don't Blame God: Reason #2

Scripture Reading
James 1:2-3

Reflection
God Uses Problems To Search Us. What tests have you faced recently? Did your response allow you to be defeated or developed?

THE TRUE VINE - REFLECTION JOURNAL 1

Day 72

Don't Blame God: Reason #3

Scripture Reading
Psalm 119:71-72

Reflection
God Uses Problems To Chastise Us. It's those stern life lessons that often teach us the most. What important life lesson have you had to learn the hard way?

THE TRUE VINE - REFLECTION JOURNAL 1

Day 73

Don't Blame God: Reason #4

Scripture Reading
Psalm 61:4; 91:1-2

Reflection
God Uses Problems To Shelter Us. Problems can be blessings in disguise. Have you ever had a moment when you thought to yourself "that could have been me"? Reflect and journal about that moment.

THE TRUE VINE - REFLECTION JOURNAL 1

Day 74

Don't Blame God: Reason #5

Scripture Reading
Romans 5:3-4

Reflection
God Uses Problems To Bring Us To Maturity. Have you ever gone through something tough; yet, ultimately were glad you went through it? How did God build your character through that experience?

THE TRUE VINE - REFLECTION JOURNAL 1

Day 75

Letters To God

Scripture Reading
Psalm 57:2-3; 106:44

Reflection
Write your own prayer to God. Tell Him what's on your heart.

THE TRUE VINE - REFLECTION JOURNAL 1

Day 76

How To Pray

Scripture Reading
Luke 11:1-4

Reflection

Remember the things that Jesus outlined as important and make them important in your prayer life as well. Journal your prayers, and with time you will begin to see how your prayer language grows. You'll also see how God has moved in your life and which prayers have been answered as time has passed.

THE TRUE VINE - REFLECTION JOURNAL 1

Day 77

Meditation For The Soul

Scripture Reading
Joshua 1:8 and Psalm 1:2; 19:14

Reflection
Let the word of God be your source of wisdom and direction. Strive towards living a godly life, and because of your obedience, you will prosper and succeed. Will you commit today to starting a regular meditative routine?

THE TRUE VINE - REFLECTION JOURNAL 1

Day 78

12 Ordinary Men - Philip

Scripture Reading
Mark 2:17 and Matthew 10:1-4 and John 6:5-12

Reflection
The disciples are prime examples of how God can and will work through any person who is willing to do the work of God. Are you a willing vessel? If so, how have you allowed God to use you? If not, will you choose today to allow God to work through you?

THE TRUE VINE - REFLECTION JOURNAL 1

Day 79

Declare and Decree - You Are Forgiven

Scripture Reading
Psalm 103:2-5, 12

Reflection
Write your own declaration, and speak it over your life.

THE TRUE VINE - REFLECTION JOURNAL 1

Day 80

Pray For Healing

Scripture Reading
James 5:15-16 and Isaiah 53:5

Reflection
We have the power, through prayer, to heal our bruised nation. Will you dedicate yourself to becoming a prayer warrior for our nation? Start praying today.

THE TRUE VINE - REFLECTION JOURNAL 1

DANENA L. WILLIAMS

Day 81

Fruits Of The Spirit - Gentleness

Scripture Reading
Galatians 5:22-23 and Philippians 4:5

Reflection
The world will be a better place when we all remember to handle each other gently. In the future, how do you plan to treat people with gentleness?

THE TRUE VINE - REFLECTION JOURNAL 1

DANENA L. WILLIAMS

Day 82

Lord, Have Mercy

Scripture Reading
Matthew 5:8; 20:29-34

Reflection
Follow Jesus' lead. Show mercy every chance you get. Actively look for situations in which you can be merciful towards another. Journal about those experiences.

THE TRUE VINE - REFLECTION JOURNAL 1

Day 83

Letters To God

Scripture Reading
Psalm 31:1-4

Reflection
Write your own prayer to God. Tell Him what's on your heart.

THE TRUE VINE - REFLECTION JOURNAL 1

Day 84

Priorities

Scripture Reading
John 17

Reflection
Write a list of what your top five priorities were before reading today's study. Then write a new list showing how you plan to change or rearrange your priorities.

THE TRUE VINE - REFLECTION JOURNAL 1

Day 85

One Touch

Scripture Reading
Mark 5:25-34

Reflection
It is by your Faith that you receive exactly what you need. What will you believe God for today?

THE TRUE VINE - REFLECTION JOURNAL 1

Day 86

Declare and Decree - You Are Motivated, Determined, And Purpose Driven

Scripture Reading
Proverbs 13:19 and Psalm 20:4

Reflection
Write your own declaration, and speak it over your life.

THE TRUE VINE - REFLECTION JOURNAL 1

Day 87

Chosen

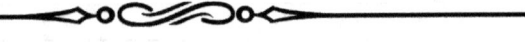

Scripture Reading
1 Samuel 16-17

Reflection
Will you believe God, today, for what needs to be done tomorrow? What task/s has God chosen you for?

THE TRUE VINE - REFLECTION JOURNAL 1

Day 88

12 Ordinary Men - Matthias

Scripture Reading
Mark 2:17 and Matthew 10:1-4 and Luke 10:1 and Acts 1:23-26

Reflection
The disciples are prime examples of how God can and will work through any person who is willing to do the work of God. Are you a willing vessel? If so, how have you allowed God to use you? If not, will you choose today to allow God to work through you?

THE TRUE VINE - REFLECTION JOURNAL 1

Day 89

Fruits Of The Spirit - Self Control

Scripture Reading
Galatians 5:22-23 and 1 Corinthians 9:24-25

Reflection
We must consciously make the decision to exercise self control at all times. When was the last time you lost control? What happened? Why? In hindsight, how could you have exercised self control in the situation?

THE TRUE VINE - REFLECTION JOURNAL 1

Day 90

All Money, Ain't Good Money

Scripture Reading
Proverbs 17:17; 18:24 and John 15:13

Reflection
Spend some time in quiet reflection over God's word for you today. Evaluate your friend list. Then, decide who you should let go and who's worth holding on to.

THE TRUE VINE - REFLECTION JOURNAL 1

More Titles by Author Danena L. Williams

Coming Soon

The True Vine - Devotional Book 2 and Reflection Journal 2

"Another powerful 90 days of reflection on God's everlasting word."

Jesus 911

"Promises From God For Every Situation"